By Ernest L. Thayer

Illustrated by C. F. Payne

Simon & Schuster Books for Young Readers

New York   London   Toronto   Sydney   Singapore

SIMON & SCHUSTER BOOKS FOR YOUNG READERS

An imprint of Simon & Schuster Children's Publishing Division

1230 Avenue of the Americas, New York, New York 10020

Book design by Billy Kelly and Mark Siegel

The text for this book is set in Wade Sans.

The illustrations for this book are rendered in acrylics, watercolor, ink, oils, and colored pencils on cold press

illustration board.

Manufactured in China

10 9 8 7 6 5 4 3 2 1

Library of Congress Cataloging-in-Publication Data

Thayer, Ernest Lawrence, 1863-1940.

Casey at the bat : a ballad of the republic sung in the year 1888 /

Ernest L. Thayer ; illlustrated by C.F. Payne.

p. cm.

ISBN 0-689-85494-3

1. Baseball players——Juvenile poetry. 2. Baseball——Juvenile poetry. 3. Children's poetry, American.

[1. Baseball——Poetry. 2. American poetry.] I. Payne, C. F., ill. II. Title.

PS3014.T3 C3 2003

811'.52——dc21

2002003472

For all those who aren't afraid to strike out and are still willing to bat

—C. F. P.

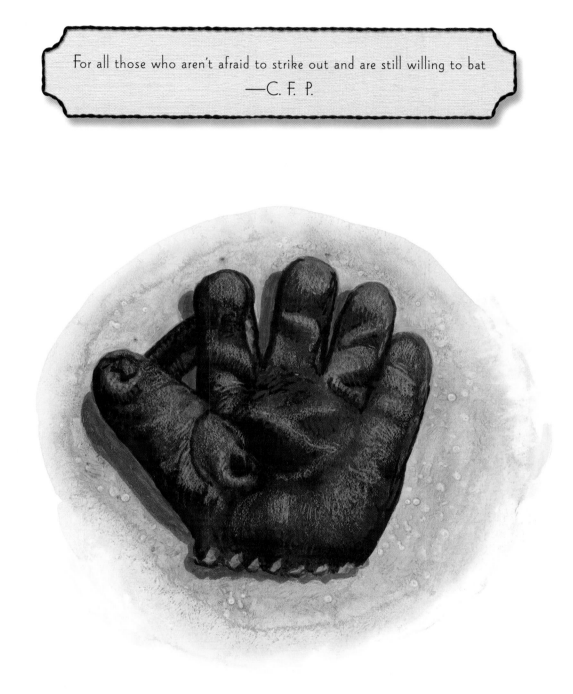

he outlook wasn't brilliant for the Mudville nine that day;

The score stood four to two with but one inning more to play.

And then when Cooney died at first, and Barrows did the same,

A sickly silence fell upon the patrons of the game.

Clung to that hope which springs eternal in the human breast;

They thought if only Casey could but get a whack at that—

We'd put up even money now with Casey at the bat.

But Flynn preceded Casey, as did also Jimmy Blake,

And the former was a lulu and the latter was a cake;

So upon that stricken multitude grim melancholy sat,

For there seemed but little chance of Casey's getting to the bat.

But Flynn let drive a single, to the wonderment of all,

And Blake, the much despised, tore the cover off the ball;

And when the dust had lifted, and the men saw what had occurred,

There was Johnnie safe at second and Flynn a-hugging third.

Then from 5,000 throats and more there rose a lusty yell;

It rumbled through the valley, it rattled in the dell;

It knocked upon the mountain and recoiled upon the flat,

For Casey, mighty Casey, was advancing to the bat.

here was ease in Casey's manner as he stepped into his place;

There was pride in Casey's bearing and a smile on Casey's face.

And when, responding to the cheers, he lightly doffed his hat,

No stranger in the crowd could doubt 'twas Casey at the bat.

en thousand eyes were on him as he rubbed his hands with dirt;

Five thousand tongues applauded when he wiped them on his shirt.

Then while the writhing pitcher ground the ball into his hip,

Defiance gleamed in Casey's eye, a sneer curled Casey's lip.

nd now the leather-covered sphere came hurtling through the air,

And Casey stood a-watching it in haughty grandeur there.

Close by the sturdy batsman the ball unheeded sped—

"That ain't my style," said Casey. "Strike one," the umpire said.

From the benches, black with people, there went up a muffled roar,

Like the beating of the storm waves on a stern and distant shore.

"Kill him! Kill the umpire!" shouted someone on the stand;

And it's likely they'd have killed him had not Casey raised his hand.

ith a smile of Christian charity great Casey's visage shone,

He stilled the rising tumult; he bade the game go on;

He signaled to the pitcher, and once more the spheroid flew;

But Casey still ignored it, and the umpire said, "Strike two."

"Fraud!" cried the maddened thousands, and echo answered, "Fraud!"

But one scornful look from Casey and the audience was awed.

They saw his face grow stern and cold, they saw his muscles strain,

And they knew that Casey wouldn't let that ball go by again.

The sneer is gone from Casey's lip, his teeth are clenched in hate;

He pounds with cruel violence his bat upon the plate.

And now the pitcher holds the ball, and now he lets it go,

And now the air is shattered by the force of Casey's blow.

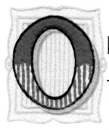Oh, somewhere in this favored land the sun is shining bright;

The band is playing somewhere, and somewhere hearts are light,

And somewhere men are laughing, and somewhere children shout;

But there is no joy in Mudville——mighty Casey has struck out.

Ernest L. Thayer was born in Lawrence, Massachusetts, on August 14, 1863. He grew up in nearby Worcester, attended Harvard College, and worked at the *San Francisco Daily Examiner*. He wrote news stories, editorials, and ballads as well as a humorous column that he signed with the nickname "Phin."

In February 1888 Thayer returned to the East Coast to join the family's wool manufacturing business. Three months later he sat down and wrote "Casey."

He sent it to the *Examiner*, where on June 3, 1888, it was printed on the editorial page and signed "Phin." Readers interpreted Thayer's "Mudville nine" as the California League club that had sunk to the bottom of the League standings. Three of the characters in the poem—Blake, Cooney, and Flynn—were the names of three well-known California League players.

After the ballad was printed in the *Examiner* it was read on the East Coast by Jim Kennedy, editor of the *New York Sporting Times*. Kennedy substituted Boston star Mike Kelly's last name for "Casey," and "Boston" for "Mudville," then cut the first five stanzas and published "Kelly at the Bat" in the July 28, 1888, issue.

But the person who really made the poem famous was a comedian named De Wolf Hopper. After receiving a clipping of the original poem from a close friend and author, Archibald Clavering Gunter, he recited the poem during a performance in New York at the Wallack Theater on August 14, 1888. The New York Giants and Chicago White Stockings players attended the show. With such an enthusiastic audience the poem became an immediate success and afterward was performed by Hopper both onstage and over the radio more than ten thousand times during the next forty years.

As the ballad became immortalized, various people claimed authorship and demanded that Hopper pay them royalties. But Hopper refused and it was not until Thayer attended one of Hopper's performances in Worcester that the matter of authorship was settled. Thayer sent a note backstage, requesting a meeting, and gave Hopper the rights to continue performing the poem without paying any royalties.

As Hopper wrote in his memoirs, "It is as perfect an epitome of our national game today as it was when every player drank his coffee from a mustache cup. There are one or more Caseys in every league, bush or big, and there is no day in the playing season that this same supreme tragedy, as stark as Aristophanes [sic] for the moment, does not befall on some field."